PIANO · VOCAL · GUITAR

THE GREAT DIVAS

ISBN 1-57560-472-8

Visit our website at www.cherrylane.com

From a Distance

As recorded by Bette Midler

Words and Music by
Julie Gold

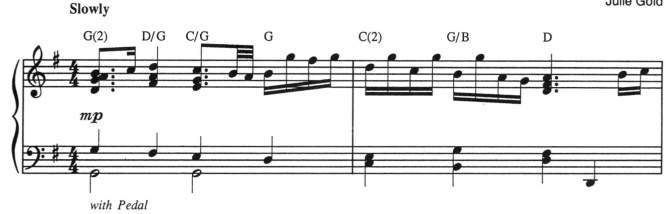

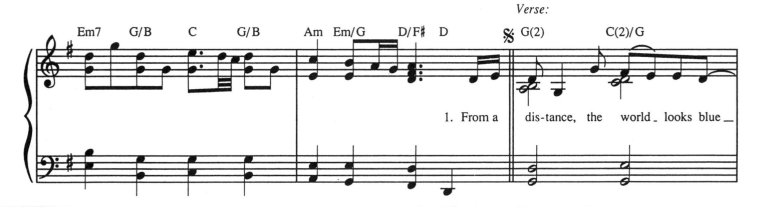

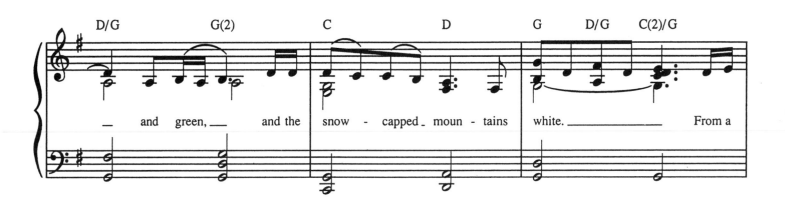

Verse 2:
From a distance, we all have enough,
And no one is in need.
There are no guns, no bombs, no diseases,
No hungry mouths to feed.
From a distance, we are instruments
Marching in a common band;
Playing songs of hope, playing songs of peace,
They're the songs of every man.
(To Bridge:)

Verse 3:
From a distance, you look like my friend
Even though we are at war.
From a distance I just cannot comprehend
What all this fighting is for.
From a distance there is harmony
And it echos through the land.
It's the hope of hopes, it's the love of loves.
It's the heart of every man.

Gypsys, Tramps and Thieves

As recorded by Cher

Words and Music by
Robert Stone

never had school-in' but he taught me well with his smooth south-ern style. _____ But

three months la-ter I'm a gal in trou-ble and I have-n't seen him for a while. _____

Mm, mm, I have-n't seen him for a

while. 3. She was down.

D.S. and fade

11

Get Closer

As recorded by Linda Rondstadt

Words and Music by
Jon Carroll

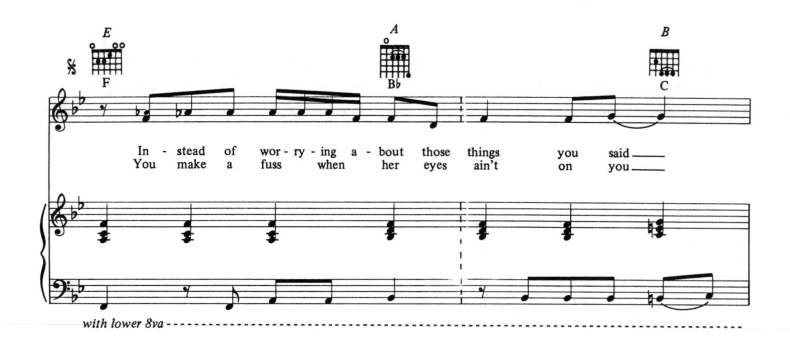

In - stead of wor - ry - ing a - bout those things you said ___
You make a fuss when her eyes ain't on you ___

with lower 8va -

Fol - low your heart ___ and for - get your head. ___
Well, give her some - thing to look for - ward to. ___

- -

May - be some - thing will jump out your mouth ___
Re - mem - ber all those oth - er girls who ran ___

- -

To make her no - tice that you're cra - zy a - bout her. Want
A - way from some - thing they didn't un - der - stand. You want

love?   Get   clos - er.   You   want
love?   Get   clos - er.   You   want

love?   Get   clos - er.
love?   Get

clos - er.

You want

love?

Get

Why you wor-ry-ing a-bout those things you said?
Oh, slide on o - ver on the seat,

I Feel The Earth Move

As recorded by Carole King

Words and Music by
Carole King

I FEEL THE EARTH MOVE

Words and Music by
CAROLE KING

The original recording contains two separate piano parts. For this arrangement, they have been combined to be playable as a solo.

I'm Every Woman

As recorded by Whitney Houston

Words and Music by
Nickolas Ashford and Valerie Simpson

ly._____ 'Cause I'm_____ ev-ery wom-an, it's all in me._____

It's_ all in me,_____

Moderate dance beat

yeah!

I'm ev - ery wom - an, it's all in me.

An - y - thing you want done, ba - by, I'll do it nat - 'ral - ly.

I'm ev - ery wom - an, it's all in me. I can read your thoughts right now, ev - ery one from A to Z.

I

I'll do it nat - 'ral - ly._____

I'm ev - ery wom - an, it's all__ in

me.__ I can read your thoughts right now, ev - ery one from A__ to Z.__

Additional Lyrics

2. I can sense your needs like rain unto the seeds.
I can make a rhyme of confusion in your mind.
And when it comes down to some good old-fashioned love,
I've got it, I've got it, I've got it, got it, baby, 'cause...
(To Chorus)

Last Dance

As recorded by Donna Summer

Words and Music by
Paul Jabara

Let's Make Love

As recorded by Faith Hill

Words and Music by
Bill Luther, Aimee Mayo,
Chris Lindsey and Marv Green

Let's Stay Together

As recorded by Tina Turner

Words and Music by
Al Green, Willie Mitchell
and Al Jackson, Jr.

Moderately fast

Let me say that since, _____ babe,

since we've been to- geth - er, ooh, __ lov - ing you for-

ev - er is all I ___ need. _____

* Recorded a half step lower.

py or sad.

Why? Oh, tell me. Why do peo-ple break up,

oh, then turn a-round and make up? I just came

to see you'd nev-er

do that _ to me. _____ I want you ba - by, 'cause

being _____ a - round you _ is all I see. _____

So ba - by, let's! _____

We ought - ta stay to - geth - er. _____

Man of La Mancha

(I, Don Quixote)
from MAN OF LA MANCHA

As recorded by Linda Eder

Lyric by Joe Darion

Music by Mitch Leigh

Moderately fast

Hear me

now, oh—— thou bleak and un-bear-a-ble world, thou art
heath-ens—— and wiz-ards and ser-pents—— of sin, all your

base and____ de - bauched as can be.____ And a
das - tard - ly do - ings are past.____ For a

knight with____ his ban - ners all brave - ly____ un - furled now
ho - ly____ en - deav - or is now to____ be - gin, and

hurls down____ his gaunt - let to thee!____ I am
vir - tue____ shall tri - umph at last!____ I am

I, Don____ Qui - xo - te, the Lord of____ La Man - cha, de -
I, Don____ Qui - xo - te, the Lord of____ La Man - cha; a

53

Misty

As recorded by Sarah Vaughan

Words by Johnny Burke

Music by Erroll Garner

Slow Ballad

with pedal

A tempo

Cmaj7 Am7

Dm9 G13 Cmaj7 Gm7 C7♭9

Look _____ at me, _____ I'm as help-less as a kit-ten _____ up a

Fmaj7 Fm9 B♭13

tree. And I feel like I'm cling-ing to a cloud, I

New Words

As recorded by Andrea Marcovicci

Words and Music by
Maury Yeston

playing starry-eyed games,
who would think it astounds us,
simply naming their names?
Turn your eyes from the

Someone Like You

from JEKYLL & HYDE

As recorded by Linda Eder

Words by Leslie Bricusse

Music by Frank Wildhorn

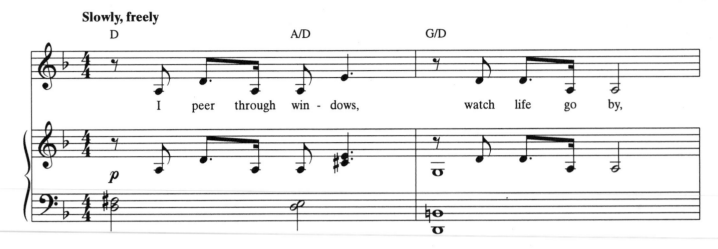

I peer through win-dows, watch life go by,

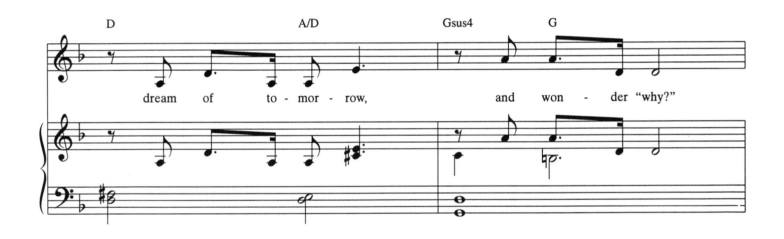

dream of to-mor-row, and won-der "why?"

The past is hold-ing me, keep-ing life at bay.

feel so a - live,_____ if some - one like you_____ found me!

So man - y se - crets I long to share! All I have need - ed is some - one there to help me see a world

ev - er be the same! There'd be a new way to live____ a

new life to love,____ if some - one like you____ found

me! Oh, if some - one____ like you found

some - one____ like me, then sud - den - ly_____ noth - ing would

Take the "A" Train

As recorded by Ella Fitzgerald

Words and Music by
Billy Strayhorn

com - ing! _____ Lis - ten _____ to those rails a -

thrum - ming. _____ All __ a - board! __ Get on the "A" __

_____ train. _____ Soon you will be on Sug - ar Hill in

Har - lem. _____

D.S. al Fine

The Way We Were

As recorded by Barbra Streisand

Words by
Alan and Marilyn Bergman

Music by Marvin Hamlisch

79

Can it be that it was all so sim- ple then, or has time re- writ- ten ev- 'ry

line? If we had the chance to do it all a- gain, tell me

would we?_____ Could we?_____ Mem - 'ries_____

_____ may be beau- ti- ful, and yet, what's too pain- ful to re-

What a Girl Wants

As recorded by Christina Aguilera

Words and Music by
Shelly Peiken and Guy Roche

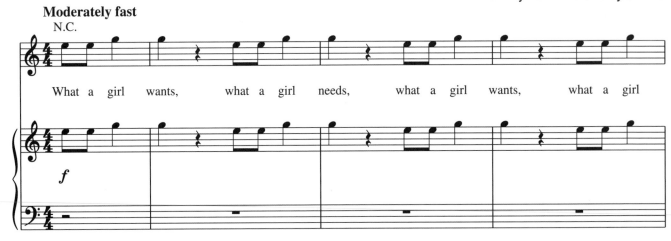

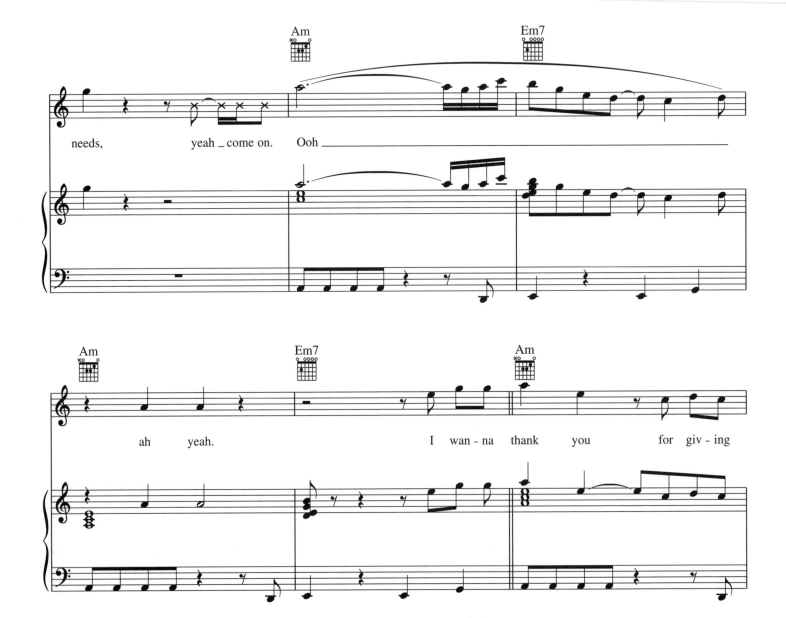

luck-y for me ___ you un - der - stand: ___ What a girl wants, (yeah) what a girl

needs (yeah) what-ev-er makes ___ me hap-py sets ___ you free. ___ And I'm

thank-ing you ___ for know-ing ex - act-ly what a girl wants, what a girl needs,

what-ev-er keeps ___ me in ___ your arms, ___ and I'm thank-ing you ___ for

When You Believe
(From The Prince of Egypt)
As recorded by Whitney Houston and Mariah Carey

Words and Music Composed by Stephen Schwartz
with Additional Music by Babyface

You____ will____ when____ you____ be-lieve.____

They don't al-ways hap-pen when____ you____ ask.____

____ And it's eas-y to give in____ to your fear.____

____ But when____ you're blind-ed by____ your pain, can't see____

94

your way clear through the rain, a small but still re-sil-ient voice says

help is ver-y near.

There can be mir-a-cles, when you be-lieve.

Though hope is frail, it's hard to kill. Who knows what mir-a-cles

you can a-chieve? When you be-lieve, some-how you will,

now you will. You will when you be - lieve._____

Bmaj7
Tacet
_____ You____ will____ when you, you will when you_____ be -

lieve, just be - lieve, just be -

lieve. You will when you be - lieve._____

96

Why Oh Why

As recorded by Celine Dion

Words and Music by
Marti Sharron and Danny Sembello

Don't you know that you're my rea - son
How can you tell me it was noth - ing, 'cause you

for my love, my life, my be - ing so se - cure and so
took a - way ev - 'ry - thing I dreamed in. Just a night when I held

*Recorded a half step higher.

damn sure.__ My heart would sure-ly die__ with-out you.__
you tight, and you know you were__ sleep-ing__ in her bed. }

1. 2. I tried to swal-low my__ pride,__ but I felt my heart__ start to trem-
3. qui-et-ly leave__ through the__ door,__ or may-be pre-tend__ the way things__

ble in-side. Wish I did-n't know__ 'cause I can't__ let you go.__ Tell me why,__
were once__ be-fore when I met__ you. I'll nev-er for-get__ you. So why,__

why when I looked__ in your eyes__

A Whiter Shade of Pale

As recorded by Sarah Brightman

Words and Music by
Keith Reid and Gary Brooker

that her face, at first __ just ghost - ly, turned a whit -

er _____ shade of pale. _____

one of six - teen ___ ves - tal vir - gins

who were leav - ing for ___ the coast. ___

And al - though my eyes were

o - pen, ___ they might just as well've ___ been closed. ___

And so it

Wonder

As recorded by Natalie Merchant

Words and Music by
Natalie Merchant

1. Doc - tors have come ___ from dis - tant cit - ies just to see ___
2. News - pap - ers ___ ask ___ in - tim - ate ques - tion, want con - fes -

Ooh _____

I _____ be - lieve

fate ___ smiled ___ and des - ti-

ny laughed as she came to my cra - dle,

110

(You Make Me Feel Like)
A Natural Woman

As recorded by Aretha Franklin

Words and Music by
Gerry Goffin, Carole King
and Jerry Wexler

feel, _____ you make _ me feel, _____ you make _ me

feel like a nat - u - ral _____ wom - an. (Wom - an.) _____

When my soul was in the lost and found, _

you came a - long to claim _____ it.

I did-n't know just what was wrong with me ____

till your kiss helped me ____ name it.

Now I'm no long-er doubt-ful

of what I'm liv-in' for. ____ And if I make ya hap-py